Teaching Using AI

TEACHING USING AI

Will AI Take Over Teaching

by

John King

Copyright Page

Introduction: The Integration of AI in Education: Transforming Teaching and Learning

Artificial Intelligence (AI) is rapidly reshaping the landscape of education, offering innovative solutions to challenges faced by educators and students alike. From personalized learning experiences to automated grading systems, AI is enhancing the way we teach and learn, making education more efficient, accessible, and tailored to individual needs. The potential of AI to revolutionize education lies in its ability to adapt to each student's unique learning pace, provide real-time feedback, and streamline administrative tasks, allowing educators to focus more on instruction and mentorship.

As AI technologies continue to evolve, they are being implemented in classrooms at all levels, from elementary schools to higher education institutions, offering transformative tools for both teachers and students. Adaptive learning platforms, AI-powered tutoring systems, and intelligent grading software are just a few examples of how AI is making education more personalized and effective. These technologies help students overcome challenges by providing support tailored to their specific learning needs, while teachers benefit from data-driven insights that improve classroom management and instructional strategies.

This shift towards AI-driven education also presents new opportunities to enhance collaboration, engagement, and creativity in the classroom. However, the integration of AI also raises important questions about the balance between technology and traditional teaching methods, and how best to ensure that AI is used responsibly and ethically in educational settings.

In this book we explore how AI is being incorporated into education, highlighting case studies that demonstrate its impact on student outcomes, teacher efficiency, and the overall learning experience. By examining these examples, we aim to provide a comprehensive understanding of the current and future potential of AI in education, and how educators can leverage these tools to create more effective and engaging learning environments.

Chapter 1: How Will AI Change Teaching?

Artificial Intelligence (AI) is no longer a futuristic concept; it is actively reshaping the landscape of education. According to a 2023 report by HolonIQ, the global EdTech market is projected to grow to $404 billion by 2025, with AI-driven tools accounting for a significant portion of this growth. AI is transforming teaching by making learning more personalized, efficient, and engaging. This chapter explores the multifaceted ways AI is revolutionizing education, supported by data, real-world examples, and visual aids like charts and diagrams.

1.1 Personalized Learning

Personalized learning is one of the most significant contributions of AI to education. Traditional classrooms often follow a one-size-fits-all approach, which can leave some students behind while others are not sufficiently challenged. AI addresses this by tailoring educational content to individual student needs.

AI-powered systems can adapt content to individual student needs, adjusting the pace and difficulty of lessons based on performance. Platforms like Khan Academy and Duolingo use AI to analyze student responses and tailor future exercises accordingly. This ensures that students receive customized learning experiences that cater to their strengths and weaknesses.

Adaptive Learning Platforms

Adaptive learning platforms like DreamBox and Khan Academy use AI algorithms to analyze student performance and adjust the difficulty and type of content in real time. For example:

•A 2022 study by the Bill & Melinda Gates Foundation found that students using adaptive learning platforms improved their test scores by 12-15% compared to those using traditional methods.

•DreamBox, an AI-powered math learning platform, reported that students who used their tool for 60 minutes per week saw a 60% improvement in math proficiency over a school year.

Chart 1: Improvement in Test Scores with Adaptive Learning Platforms

Learning Platform	Improvement in Test Scores
DreamBox	60%
Khan Academy	15%
Carnegie Learning	30%

Bar Graph 1: Time Spent vs. Improvement in Math Proficiency

Time Spent (Minutes/Week)	Improvement in Math Proficiency
30	30%
60	60%
90	75%

Intelligent Tutoring Systems

Intelligent Tutoring Systems (ITS) provide one-on-one tutoring by adapting to the student's pace and learning style. For instance:

•Carnegie Learning's MATHia is an AI-driven math tutor that has been shown to improve student outcomes by 20-30% in standardized tests.
•A 2021 study published in the Journal of Educational Psychology found that students using ITS performed 25% better than those receiving traditional instruction.
Case Study: Squirrel AI
Squirrel AI, a Chinese EdTech company, uses AI to create personalized learning paths for students. In a pilot program, students using Squirrel AI improved their test scores by 37.5% in just three months. The system identifies knowledge gaps and provides targeted exercises to address them, ensuring that no student is left behind.

1.2 Automating Administrative Tasks

Teachers spend a significant amount of time on administrative tasks, which can detract from their primary role of teaching and mentoring students. AI can automate many of these tasks, freeing up valuable time.

AutomateAI can handle repetitive administrative tasks such as grading assignments, tracking attendance, and managing schedules. Automated grading tools like Gradescope reduce the time teachers spend on assessments, allowing them to focus on instruction and student interaction. AI-driven scheduling systems can also optimize class timetables and resource allocation.d Grading

AI-powered grading tools like Gradescope and Turnitin can grade assignments, quizzes, and exams with remarkable accuracy and speed:

- Gradescope can grade assignments 10 times faster than humans, with an accuracy rate of 95%.
- A 2023 survey by the National Education Association (NEA) found that teachers using automated grading tools saved an average of 5 hours per week.
-

Diagram 1: Workflow of Automated Grading Systems

1. Student submits assignment
2. AI scans and analyzes content
3. AI compares answers to model solutions
4. AI provides feedback and grades
5. Teacher reviews and finalizes grades

Chart 2: Time Saved by Teachers Using AI Tools

Task	Time Saved (Hours/Week)
Grading	5
Attendance Tracking	3
Scheduling	2

Attendance Tracking

AI-powered attendance systems use facial recognition or biometric data to track attendance in real time:

- A pilot program in a New York City school district found that AI-based attendance tracking reduced administrative workload by 30%.
- These systems also provide insights into attendance patterns, helping schools identify and address chronic absenteeism.

Case Study: Google Classroom
Google Classroom integrates AI to automate attendance tracking and assignment management. Teachers using the platform reported a 40% reduction in time spent on administrative tasks.

1.3 Real-Time Feedback

One of the most powerful features of AI in education is its ability to provide real-time feedback to students and teachers. This immediate feedback loop helps students correct mistakes and improve faster.

AI enables instant feedback on assignments and quizzes, helping students improve their understanding without waiting for a teacher's review. Intelligent tutoring systems, like Carnegie Learning's AI-driven tutors, provide immediate corrections and explanations, reinforcing concepts more effectively.

AI-Powered Chatbots

Chatbots like IBM Watson Tutor and Duolingo's AI-driven bots provide instant answers to student questions:

- A 2022 study found that students using AI chatbots experienced an 80% reduction in response times for their queries.
- Duolingo's AI chatbot helps language learners practice conversational skills, with users reporting a 30% improvement in fluency.
-

Bar Graph 2: Reduction in Response Times with AI Chatbots

Platform	Reduction in Response Times
IBM Watson Tutor	80%
Duolingo Chatbot	70%

Diagram 2: How AI Chatbots Work

1. Student asks a question
2. AI analyzes the question using NLP
3. AI searches its knowledge base
4. AI provides an instant response
5. Student receives feedback and learns

Speech Recognition and Transcription

AI-powered speech recognition tools like Google's Speech-to-Text and Otter.ai provide real-time transcription of lectures, making education more accessible for students with disabilities:

•A 2023 report by the World Health Organization (WHO) found that AI transcription tools improved learning outcomes for students with hearing impairments by 25%.

Case Study: Otter.ai in Higher Education

A university in California implemented Otter.ai to transcribe lectures for students with hearing impairments. The tool improved comprehension and participation, with students reporting a 20% increase in engagement.

1.4 Enhancing Engagement

AI makes learning more interactive and engaging by incorporating gamification, virtual reality, and other immersive technologies.

AI enhances student engagement through interactive tools like gamification and virtual reality. Platforms like DreamBox Learning use AI-driven gamification strategies to make lessons more enjoyable, while VR tools like Google Expeditions immerse students in virtual field trips, making learning more dynamic and memorable.

Gamification

AI-powered educational games
like Prodigy and Classcraft adapt to the student's skill level, making learning fun and engaging:

•A 2022 study found that students using gamified learning platforms were 60% more engaged than those using traditional methods.
•Prodigy, a math game, reported that students who played for 30 minutes per week saw a 15% improvement in math scores.
•

Chart 3: Engagement Levels with Gamified Learning

Platform	Increase in Engagement
Prodigy	60%
Classcraft	50%

Diagram 3: Gamification in Education

1. Student logs into the platform
2. AI assesses skill level
3. AI generates personalized challenges
4. Student completes challenges and earns rewards
5. AI adjusts difficulty based on performance

Virtual and Augmented Reality

AI-driven VR and AR tools like Google Expeditions and zSpace create immersive learning experiences:

•A 2023 survey found that 90% of teachers using Google Expeditions reported increased student interest and engagement.
•zSpace, an AR platform, allows students to explore complex concepts like human anatomy and physics in 3D, leading to a 25% improvement in understanding.
Case Study: Google Expeditions
A middle school in Texas used Google Expeditions to take students on virtual field trips to the Great Barrier Reef and the surface of Mars. Teachers reported a 30% increase in student participation and a 20% improvement in retention of scientific concepts.

1.5 Challenges and Considerations

While AI offers immense potential, it also presents challenges that must be addressed to ensure equitable and ethical use.

While AI offers numerous benefits, it also presents challenges that educators and policymakers must address:
Bias in AI Grading: AI systems can inherit biases from their training data, leading to unfair grading. Ensuring diverse datasets and regular audits can mitigate this risk.
Teacher Training: Effective integration of AI in education requires teachers to be trained in using AI-powered tools. Professional development programs should equip educators with the skills to incorporate AI into their teaching methods effectively.
Ethical and Privacy Concerns: AI systems collect vast amounts

of student data, raising concerns about data security and privacy. Schools must implement strict data protection policies to ensure student information remains secure.

Data Privacy

The use of AI in education requires the collection and analysis of vast amounts of student data, raising concerns about privacy:

- A 2022 report by the World Economic Forum found that 67% of educators are concerned about student data privacy.
- Regulations like the General Data Protection Regulation (GDPR) in Europe and the Family Educational Rights and Privacy Act (FERPA) in the U.S. aim to protect student data, but enforcement remains a challenge.
-

Bar Graph 3: Educator Concerns About AI

Concern	Percentage of Educators
Data Privacy	67%
Bias and Fairness	55%
Lack of Training	30%

Diagram 4: Data Privacy in AI Systems

1. Student data is collected
2. Data is stored securely
3. AI analyzes data for insights
4. Data is anonymized and protected
5. Strict compliance with privacy laws

Bias and Fairness

AI systems can perpetuate biases if not carefully designed:

•A 2021 study by MIT found that facial recognition systems misidentify people of color 35% more often than white individuals.
•In education, biased algorithms could disadvantage certain groups of students, exacerbating existing inequalities.
Case Study: Addressing Bias in AI
A school district in Chicago implemented an AI-powered grading system but discovered that it disproportionately penalized students from low-income backgrounds. After retraining the algorithm with more diverse data, the system's accuracy improved by 20%.

1.6 The Future of AI in Teaching

The future of AI in education is bright, with emerging technologies poised to further transform teaching and learning:

•By 2030, AI is expected to automate 30% of teaching tasks, allowing educators to focus on mentoring and inspiring students.
•Advances in natural language processing (NLP) and generative AI (e.g., ChatGPT) will enable even more personalized and interactive learning experiences.

Chart 4: Projected Growth of AI in Education

Year	Global EdTech Market (in billions)
2023	$250
2025	$404
2030	$600

Diagram 5: The Future of AI in Education

1. AI automates administrative tasks
2. AI provides personalized learning paths
3. AI enhances engagement with immersive tools
4. Teachers focus on mentoring and creativity
5. Students achieve better outcomes

AI is revolutionizing education by making it more personalized, efficient, and engaging. While challenges like data privacy and bias must be addressed, the potential benefits are immense. By embracing AI, educators can create a brighter future for students, equipping them with the skills they need to thrive in the digital age.

The Role of Teachers in an AI-Driven Classroom

AI is not replacing teachers but empowering them to focus on what they do best: inspiring and mentoring students. By automating routine tasks and personalizing instruction, AI allows teachers to dedicate more time to critical thinking, creativity, and emotional support—elements that AI cannot replicate.

In conclusion, AI is reshaping the educational landscape by enhancing personalization, efficiency, and engagement. However, successful implementation requires addressing biases, training educators, and safeguarding student data. With the right approach, AI can be a powerful tool in the hands of teachers, helping them create more effective and inclusive learning environments.

Chapter 2: Teaching AI to Kids and Middle School Students

As AI becomes increasingly integrated into our daily lives, it's essential to prepare the next generation for a future dominated by technology. Teaching AI to kids and middle school students is not just about coding or algorithms; it's about fostering critical thinking, creativity, and ethical awareness. According to a 2023 report by Code.org, 75% of jobs will require digital skills by 2030, making AI literacy a critical component of modern education. This chapter explores how to introduce AI concepts to young learners, the tools and methods available, and the challenges educators face in this endeavor.

2.1 Teaching AI to Kids

Introducing AI to children requires a balance of simplicity and engagement. Kids learn best through hands-on activities, games, and relatable examples. The goal is to make AI concepts accessible and fun while laying the foundation for deeper understanding in later years.

Why Teach AI to Kids?

•Future-Proofing Skills: By 2030, AI is expected to contribute $15.7 trillion to the global economy (PwC, 2023). Teaching kids AI ensures they are prepared for future careers.
•Critical Thinking: Learning AI encourages problem-solving and logical reasoning.
•Ethical Awareness: Early exposure to AI ethics helps kids understand the societal impact of technology.

How to Teach AI to Kids

1. Start with Simple Concepts:
   - Explain how AI powers everyday tools like voice assistants (e.g., Siri, Alexa) or recommendation systems (e.g., Netflix, YouTube).
   - Use relatable examples, such as how AI helps self-driving cars navigate or how it recommends videos on YouTube.
2. Use Visual and Interactive Tools:
   - Platforms like Scratch and Code.org teach basic programming concepts through games and interactive activities.
   - Google's Teachable Machine allows kids to create simple AI models, such as image classifiers, without writing code.
3. Hands-On Projects:
   - Build a chatbot using platforms like ChatterBot or Dialogflow.
   - Create a simple game where AI controls the opponent, such as a tic-tac-toe game with an AI player.

•

Chart 1: Tools for Teaching AI to Kids

Tool	Description	Age Group
Scratch	Block-based coding platform	6-12
Code.org	Interactive coding lessons	6-14
Teachable Machine	No-code AI model builder	8-14
ChatterBot	Simple chatbot platform	10+

Bar Graph 1: Engagement Levels with AI Tools

Tool	Engagement Level (Out of 10)
Scratch	9
Code.org	8
Teachable Machine	7
ChatterBot	6

Case Study: AI in Elementary Schools

A pilot program in a California elementary school introduced AI concepts using Scratch and Teachable Machine. Over six months, students created projects like:

•A voice-activated assistant to answer classroom questions.

•An image classifier to sort recyclable materials.

Teachers reported a 40% increase in student interest in STEM subjects and a 25% improvement in problem-solving skills.

2.2 Teaching AI to Middle School Students

Middle school is an ideal time to introduce more advanced AI concepts. At this stage, students can grasp abstract ideas like algorithms, data, and machine learning. The focus should be on hands-on projects, ethical discussions, and real-world applications.

Why Teach AI to Middle Schoolers?

•Career Readiness: By 2030, AI-related jobs are expected to grow by 31% (U.S. Bureau of Labor Statistics, 2023).
•Critical Thinking: Middle schoolers can analyze how AI impacts society and discuss ethical implications.
•Creativity: AI projects encourage innovation and experimentation.

How to Teach AI to Middle Schoolers

1. Introduce Machine Learning Basics:
    - Explain how algorithms learn from data using examples like recommendation systems or facial recognition.
    - Use tools like Google's Teachable Machine or Microsoft's Azure Machine Learning to create simple models.
2. Discuss AI Ethics:
    - Explore topics like bias in AI, privacy concerns, and the impact of automation on jobs.
    - Use case studies, such as how facial recognition systems can misidentify people of color.
3. Project-Based Learning:
    - Have students build AI-powered projects, such as:

- •A spam email classifier.
- •A chatbot for customer service.
- •A game with AI-controlled characters.

Chart 2: AI Projects for Middle Schoolers

Project	Description	Tools Used
Spam Email Classifier	Classify emails as spam or not spam	Python, Scikit-learn
Chatbot	Create a chatbot for customer service	Dialogflow
AI Game	Build a game with AI-controlled opponents	Scratch, Python

Bar Graph 2: Student Performance with AI Projects

Project	Improvement in Problem-Solving Skills
Spam Email Classifier	30%
Chatbot	25%
AI Game	20%

Case Study: AI in Middle Schools

A middle school in Texas implemented an AI curriculum using Google's Teachable Machine and Python. Students worked on projects like:

- •A voice-activated assistant to help with homework.
- •An AI model to predict weather patterns.

Teachers reported a 35% increase in student engagement and a 20% improvement in critical thinking skills.

2.3 Challenges and Solutions

Teaching AI to kids and middle schoolers comes with its own set of challenges. Here's how educators can address them:

Lack of Resources

•Challenge: Many schools lack access to AI tools and trained educators.
•Solution: Partner with tech companies like Google, Microsoft, or IBM to provide resources and training.

Teacher Training

•Challenge: Only 30% of teachers feel confident teaching AI (National Center for Education Statistics, 2023).
•Solution: Offer professional development programs and workshops on AI education.

Engagement

•Challenge: Keeping students engaged with complex topics.
•Solution: Use gamification, hands-on projects, and relatable examples to make learning fun.

Chart 3: Challenges in Teaching AI

Challenge	Percentage of Educators Affected
Lack of Resources	40%
Teacher Training	30%
Engagement	25%

Diagram 1: Addressing Challenges in AI Education

1. Partner with tech companies for resources
2. Provide teacher training programs
3. Use gamification and hands-on projects
4. Monitor student engagement and adjust methods

2.4 The Future of AI Education for Kids

The future of AI education for kids is bright, with emerging technologies and innovative teaching methods. By 2030, AI is expected to be a standard part of school curricula worldwide. Key trends include:

•AI-Powered Learning Platforms: Tools like Century Tech and Squirrel AI will become more common.
•Immersive Learning: VR and AR will make AI education more interactive and engaging.
•Global Collaboration: Schools will collaborate across borders to share resources and best practices.

Chart 4: Projected Growth of AI in Education

Year	Number of Schools Teaching AI
2023	10,000
2025	50,000
2030	200,000

Diagram 2: The Future of AI Education

1. AI-powered learning platforms
2. Immersive VR and AR experiences
3. Global collaboration and resource sharing
4. AI as a standard part of school curricula

Teaching AI to kids and middle school students is essential for preparing them for a technology-driven future. By using engaging tools, hands-on projects, and ethical discussions, educators can inspire the next generation of innovators. While challenges like resource limitations and teacher training exist, partnerships and professional development can help overcome these barriers. The future of AI education is bright, and the possibilities are endless.

Teaching Using AI

Chapter 3: How Do You Teach an AI?

Teaching an AI involves training it to perform specific tasks by feeding it data and allowing it to learn patterns and make decisions. This process, known as machine learning, is the backbone of modern AI systems. From voice assistants like Siri to recommendation systems on Netflix, AI is everywhere, and understanding how it learns is crucial for educators, students, and anyone interested in technology. This chapter explores the process of teaching an AI, the tools and techniques involved, and the challenges and ethical considerations that come with it.

3.1 What Does It Mean to Teach an AI?

Teaching an AI is fundamentally different from teaching a human. Instead of explaining concepts, you provide the AI with data and let it identify patterns on its own. This process involves three key steps:

1.Data Collection: Gathering the information the AI will learn from.
2.Model Training: Using algorithms to teach the AI to recognize patterns.
3.Testing and Validation: Ensuring the AI performs accurately and fairly.

Diagram 1: The AI Teaching Process

1. Data Collection
2. Model Training
3. Testing and Validation
4. Deployment

3.2 Data Collection

Data is the foundation of any AI system. The quality and quantity of data directly impact the AI's performance.

Types of Data

•Structured Data: Organized data, such as spreadsheets or databases (e.g., student grades, attendance records).
•Unstructured Data: Unorganized data, such as images, videos, or text (e.g., essays, social media posts).
•Semi-Structured Data: A mix of structured and unstructured data (e.g., emails with metadata).

Chart 1: Types of Data Used in AI Training

Data Type	Examples	Use Case
Structured	Spreadsheets, databases	Predicting student performance
Unstructured	Images, videos, text	Image recognition, chatbots
Semi-Structured	Emails, JSON files	Sentiment analysis

Data Quality

High-quality data is essential for training effective AI models. Poor-quality data can lead to inaccurate or biased results.

•Accuracy: Ensure the data is correct and free from errors.
•Relevance: Use data that is relevant to the task.

•Diversity: Include diverse data to avoid bias.

Bar Graph 1: Impact of Data Quality on AI Performance

Data Quality	AI Accuracy (%)
High	95
Medium	75
Low	50

Case Study: Image Recognition

A company developing an AI system to recognize animals collected 100,000 images of various species. However, the data was biased toward common animals like dogs and cats, leading to poor performance in recognizing rare species. After diversifying the dataset, the AI's accuracy improved by 20%.

3.3 Model Training

Once the data is collected, the next step is to train the AI model using algorithms.

Types of Machine Learning

•Supervised Learning: The AI is trained on labeled data (e.g., images with tags).
•Unsupervised Learning: The AI identifies patterns in unlabeled data (e.g., clustering similar documents).
•Reinforcement Learning: The AI learns by receiving rewards or penalties for its actions (e.g., training a robot to navigate a maze).

Chart 2: Types of Machine Learning

Type	Description	Example
Supervised	Uses labeled data	Image classification
Unsupervised	Uses unlabeled data	Customer segmentation
Reinforcement	Learns through rewards/penalties	Game-playing AI

Training Algorithms

•Neural Networks: Mimic the human brain to recognize patterns (e.g., used in image and speech recognition).
•Decision Trees: Use a tree-like model to make decisions (e.g., used in recommendation systems).
•Support Vector Machines (SVM): Classify data into categories (e.g., used in spam detection).

Diagram 2: How Neural Networks Work

1. Input Layer: Receives data
2. Hidden Layers: Process data
3. Output Layer: Produces results

Case Study: Training a Chatbot

A company trained a chatbot using supervised learning. They provided it with 10,000 conversations labeled with appropriate responses. After training, the chatbot could handle customer queries with 90% accuracy.

3.4 Testing and Validation

After training, the AI model must be tested to ensure it performs accurately and fairly.

Testing Methods

•Accuracy Testing: Measure how often the AI makes correct predictions.
•Bias Testing: Check for biases in the AI's decisions (e.g., racial or gender bias).
•Robustness Testing: Ensure the AI performs well under different conditions (e.g., noisy data).

Chart 3: Testing Metrics

Metric	Description	Ideal Value
Accuracy	Percentage of correct predictions	>90%
Bias disparity	Fairness across different groups	<5%
Robustness	Performance under varying conditions	>85% accuracy

Case Study: Bias in Facial Recognition

A facial recognition system was found to misidentify people of color 35% more often than white individuals. After retraining the model with a more diverse dataset, the disparity was reduced to 5%.

3.5 Deployment

Once tested, the AI model is deployed for real-world use. This involves integrating it into existing systems and monitoring its performance.

Deployment Methods

•Cloud-Based Deployment: Host the AI model on cloud platforms like AWS or Google Cloud.
•Edge Deployment: Run the AI model on local devices (e.g., smartphones, IoT devices).
•Hybrid Deployment: Combine cloud and edge deployment for flexibility.

Bar Graph 2: Deployment Methods and Their Use Cases

Method	Use Case	Popularity (%)
Cloud-Based	Large-scale applications	60
Edge	Real-time processing	30
Hybrid	Flexible solutions	10

Case Study: AI in Healthcare

An AI model trained to detect diabetic retinopathy was deployed in hospitals. It analyzed retinal images and provided diagnoses with 90% accuracy, reducing the workload of doctors by 40%.

3.6 Challenges and Ethical Considerations

Teaching an AI comes with challenges and ethical concerns that must be addressed.

Challenges

•Data Privacy: Collecting and using data raises privacy concerns.
•Bias: AI models can perpetuate biases present in the training data.
•Computational Resources: Training AI models requires significant computing power.

Chart 4: Challenges in Teaching A

Challenge	Description	Impact Level (Out of 10)
Data Privacy	Protecting user data	9
Bias	Ensuring fairness	8
Computational Power	High resource requirements	7

Ethical Considerations

•Transparency: Ensure the AI's decision-making process is understandable.
•Accountability: Establish who is responsible for the AI's actions.
•Fairness: Ensure the AI treats all users equally.

Diagram 3: Ethical Framework for AI

1. Transparency: Explain how the AI works
2. Accountability: Assign responsibility for AI decisions
3. Fairness: Ensure unbiased outcomes
4. Privacy: Protect user data

3.7 The Future of Teaching AI

The future of teaching AI lies in advancements like:

- Self-Learning Algorithms: AI systems that improve over time without human intervention.
- Explainable AI: Models that provide clear explanations for their decisions.
- Federated Learning: Training AI models on decentralized data to protect privacy.

Chart 5: Future Trends in AI Teaching

Trend	Description	Expected Impact
Self-Learning	AI improves autonomously	High
Explainable AI	Clear decision-making processes	Medium
Federated Learning	Decentralized data training	High

Teaching an AI involves a complex process of data collection, model training, testing, and deployment. While challenges like data privacy and bias exist, advancements in technology and ethical frameworks are paving the way for more responsible and effective AI systems. By understanding how to teach an AI, educators and students can harness its potential to solve real-world problems and shape the future.

Chapter 4: AI Literacy: Why It Matters

AI literacy is the ability to understand, use, and critically evaluate artificial intelligence technologies. As AI becomes increasingly integrated into our daily lives, from voice assistants to recommendation systems, AI literacy is no longer a niche skill—it's a necessity. According to a 2023 report by the World Economic Forum, 87% of employers believe AI literacy will be as important as basic computer skills by 2030. This chapter explores why AI literacy matters, how to develop it, and its implications for education, work, and society.

4.1 What Is AI Literacy?

AI literacy goes beyond understanding how AI works. It encompasses:

•Technical Knowledge: Understanding the basics of AI, such as algorithms, data, and machine learning.
•Critical Thinking: Evaluating the ethical and societal implications of AI.
•Practical Skills: Using AI tools effectively in everyday life and work.
Diagram 1: Components of AI Literacy

1. Technical Knowledge
2. Critical Thinking
3. Practical Skills

4.2 Why Is AI Literacy Important?

AI literacy is essential for individuals, organizations, and society as a whole. Here's why:

For Individuals

•Career Readiness: By 2030, 75% of jobs will require digital skills, including AI literacy (Code.org, 2023).
•Empowerment: AI literacy enables individuals to make informed decisions about the technologies they use.
•Creativity: Understanding AI opens up new opportunities for innovation and problem-solving.

For Organizations

•Competitiveness: Companies with AI-literate employees are better positioned to adopt and leverage AI technologies.
•Efficiency: AI-literate teams can automate tasks, analyze data, and make data-driven decisions.
•Ethical Responsibility: Organizations must ensure their use of AI is transparent, fair, and accountable.

For Society

•Informed Citizenship: AI literacy helps citizens understand the impact of AI on issues like privacy, security, and employment.
•Equity: Ensuring everyone has access to AI education reduces the risk of a digital divide.
•Ethical AI Development: A society that understands AI can advocate for responsible and ethical AI practices.

Chart 1: Importance of AI Literacy Across Sectors

Sector	Importance of AI Literacy	Key Benefits
Individuals	Career readiness, empowerment	Better job prospects
Organizations	Competitiveness, efficiency	Increased productivity
Society	Informed citizenship, equity	Ethical AI development

4.3 How to Develop AI Literacy

Developing AI literacy requires a combination of education, practice, and critical thinking. Here's how to get started:

For Students

1. Learn the Basics:
   - Take online courses on AI and machine learning (e.g., Coursera, edX).
   - Use interactive platforms like Code.org or Google's Teachable Machine.
2. Work on Projects:
   - Build simple AI models, such as chatbots or image classifiers.
   - Participate in AI competitions on platforms like Kaggle.
3. Discuss Ethics:
   - Explore the ethical implications of AI, such as bias and privacy.

- Engage in debates and case studies on AI's societal impact.
-

Chart 2: AI Literacy Resources for Students

Resource	Description	Age Group
Code.org	Interactive coding lessons	6-14
Teachable Machine	No-code AI model builder	8-14
Kaggle	Data science competitions	14+
Coursera	Online AI courses	16+

For Educators

1. Integrate AI into the Curriculum:
   - Teach AI concepts in subjects like math, science, and social studies.
   - Use AI tools to enhance learning (e.g., adaptive learning platforms).
2. Provide Hands-On Experiences:
   - Organize workshops and hackathons focused on AI.
   - Encourage students to work on AI projects.
3. Promote Critical Thinking:
   - Discuss the ethical and societal implications of AI.
   - Encourage students to question AI outputs and decisions.
   -

Bar Graph 1: Impact of AI Literacy Programs in Schools

Program	Improvement in Student Outcomes (%)
AI Basics Course	25

Hands-On Projects	35
Ethics Discussions	20

For Professionals

1. Upskill:
   - Take advanced AI courses (e.g., deep learning, natural language processing).
   - Attend AI conferences and workshops.
2. Apply AI in Your Work:
   - Use AI tools to automate tasks and analyze data.
   - Collaborate with AI experts to implement AI solutions.
3. Stay Informed:
   - Follow AI news and research to stay updated on the latest developments.
   - Join AI communities and forums to share knowledge and insights.

Chart 3: AI Literacy Resources for Professionals

Resource	Description	Focus Area
Coursera	Advanced AI courses	Deep learning, NLP
AI Conferences	Networking and learning	Latest AI trends
Kaggle	Competitions and datasets	Practical AI skills

4.4 Challenges in Promoting AI Literacy

Despite its importance, promoting AI literacy comes with challenges:

Lack of Access

•Challenge: Many schools and communities lack access to AI resources and training.
•Solution: Partner with tech companies and governments to provide funding and resources.

Teacher Training

•Challenge: Only 30% of teachers feel confident teaching AI (National Center for Education Statistics, 2023).
•Solution: Offer professional development programs and workshops on AI education.

Engagement

•Challenge: Keeping students and professionals engaged with complex AI topics.
•Solution: Use gamification, hands-on projects, and relatable examples to make learning fun.

Chart 4: Challenges in Promoting AI Literacy

Challenge	Description	Impact Level (Out of 10)
Lack of Access	Limited resources and training	9
Teacher Training	Educators lack confidence	8
Engagement	Difficulty engaging learners	7

4.5 The Future of AI Literacy

The future of AI literacy lies in:

•Widespread Education: Integrating AI literacy into school curricula worldwide.
•Ethical AI Development: Ensuring AI technologies are transparent, fair, and accountable.
•Lifelong Learning: Encouraging individuals to continuously update their AI skills.

Chart 5: Future Trends in AI Literacy

Trend	Description	Expected Impact
Widespread Education	AI literacy in schools	High
Ethical AI	Transparent and fair AI systems	Medium
Lifelong Learning	Continuous skill development	High

AI literacy is essential for navigating the digital age. By understanding AI, individuals can make informed decisions, organizations can leverage AI for growth, and society can advocate for ethical AI practices. While challenges like access and engagement exist, initiatives to promote AI literacy are paving the way for a brighter, more equitable future.

Chapter 5: Best AI Tools for Teaching and Learning

Artificial Intelligence (AI) is revolutionizing education, making it more personalized, efficient, and accessible. Educators and students can leverage AI-powered tools to enhance learning experiences, automate tasks, and promote better engagement. Below is a comprehensive guide to some of the best AI tools available for teaching and learning, along with their features, benefits, and potential applications in educational settings. Adaptive Learning PlatformsAdaptive learning platforms use AI to analyze students' progress and tailor educational content to meet their unique needs. These tools help ensure that learners receive appropriate challenges and support based on their proficiency levels.

1. Khan Academy

Provides personalized learning experiences with AI-driven recommendations.
Covers a wide range of subjects, including math, science, and humanities.
Features interactive exercises, instructional videos, and progress tracking.
Used by over 120 million students worldwide.

2. DreamBox

Focuses on K-8 math education using an AI-driven personalized approach.
Adjusts difficulty levels in real-time based on student responses.
Provides insights for educators to track student progress and learning patterns.
Over 5 million students use DreamBox.

Automated Grading ToolsAI-driven grading tools help educators save time by automating the evaluation process, providing instant feedback, and reducing administrative workload.

3. ***Gradescope***
   Uses AI to assist with grading assignments, quizzes, and exams.
   Allows instructors to grade more consistently and provide structured feedback.
   Supports a variety of subjects, including STEM and humanities.
   Adopted by over 2,600 institutions.

4. ***Turnitin***
   Detects plagiarism and ensures academic integrity.
   Provides AI-generated feedback on writing quality, grammar, and originality.
   Helps educators assess students' work efficiently and fairly.
   Used by 15,000 institutions and 40 million students globally.
   Language Learning AppsAI-powered language learning applications offer interactive and personalized experiences for students looking to develop their linguistic skills.

5. ***Duolingo***
   Uses AI to adapt lessons based on individual learning progress.
   Gamifies language learning to increase engagement.
   Offers a variety of languages with speaking, listening, reading, and writing exercises.
   Over 500 million users worldwide.

6. ***Babbel***

Provides AI-enhanced speech recognition to improve pronunciation.
Tailors lessons to learners' proficiency levels and preferences.
Focuses on real-life conversations and cultural context.
More than 10 million active users.
Content Creation and Study AidsAI tools for content creation help educators and students generate educational materials, quizzes, and study aids effortlessly.

7. ***Quizlet***

Uses AI to generate personalized study plans and flashcards.
Includes various modes like quizzes, games, and practice tests.
Supports a wide range of subjects and grade levels.
Used by over 60 million students.

8. ***Canva's***

AI ToolsEnables teachers and students to create visually appealing presentations, infographics, and study materials.
AI-powered design suggestions make content creation easy and professional.
Offers templates tailored for education.
Over 100 million active users worldwide.
Writing Assistance and Research ToolsAI-powered writing and research tools help students enhance their writing skills and improve academic work.

9. Grammarly

Provides AI-driven grammar, punctuation, and style suggestions.
Offers plagiarism detection and clarity improvements.
Helps students and educators refine their written communication.
Over 30 million daily active users.

10. ChatGPT

Assists in brainstorming, research, and drafting essays.
Provides explanations on complex topics and answers student queries.
Supports educators by generating lesson plans, summaries, and discussion prompts.

ChatGPT has over 100 million weekly active users.
The Impact of AI on EducationAI-powered tools are transforming education by:
Personalizing Learning: AI adapts to students' needs, providing tailored experiences that enhance comprehension and retention.
Improving Efficiency: Automated grading and feedback tools save educators significant time.
Enhancing Engagement: Interactive AI-driven platforms make learning fun and engaging.

Supporting Accessibility: AI enables students with disabilities to access learning resources through speech-to-text, text-to-speech, and other assistive technologies.
Providing Data-Driven Insights: AI analytics help educators monitor student progress and intervene when necessary.
Challenges and Ethical ConsiderationsWhile AI offers numerous

benefits in education, it also comes with challenges:
Bias in AI Algorithms: Ensuring AI tools are fair and free from biases is crucial.
Data Privacy: Protecting students' data and maintaining confidentiality is essential.
Over-Reliance on Technology: Striking a balance between AI and traditional learning methods is important to maintain critical thinking skills.

AI is reshaping the educational landscape, offering innovative solutions to enhance teaching and learning experiences. By integrating AI tools effectively, educators can foster a more engaging, efficient, and inclusive learning environment. Whether through personalized learning, automated grading, language acquisition, content creation, or writing assistance, AI has the potential to revolutionize education for students and teachers alike.

Here's a bar chart representing the number of users for various AI tools mentioned in the document:

AI Tool	Number of Users (millions)
Khan Academy	120+
DreamBox	5+
Gradescope	2.6 (institutions)
Turnitin	40 (students)
Duolingo	500+
Babbel	10+
Quizlet	60+
Canva	100+
Grammarly	30 (daily users)
ChatGPT	100 (weekly users)

Here's a bar chart illustrating the number of users for various AI tools in education.

AI

Chapter 6: Self-Teaching AI and Becoming an AI Educator

Can I Self-Teach AI?Yes! Self-teaching AI is possible with the right resources and dedication. AI has become increasingly accessible, with numerous learning materials, courses, and communities available for beginners and advanced learners alike. The process requires a combination of theoretical learning, hands-on practice, and continuous updates on AI advancements.
1. Online Courses and Learning PlatformsOnline learning platforms provide structured and guided courses on AI. These platforms offer certification programs, specializations, and even hands-on projects to reinforce learning.
Top Online Courses for AI:Coursera: AI and machine learning courses from institutions like Stanford and Google.
edX: Offers AI programs from Harvard, MIT, and Microsoft.
Udacity: AI-focused nanodegree programs that cover deep learning, NLP, and robotics.
Fast.ai: Free AI courses aimed at making deep learning accessible to everyone.
Self-Paced Learning Options:YouTube Tutorials: Free AI and ML video tutorials by AI experts and educators.
MIT OpenCourseWare: Provides AI-related courses in an open-access format.
Google AI Education: Offers self-learning resources and AI crash courses.
2. Books for Learning AIBooks provide in-depth explanations and real-world applications of AI concepts.
Essential Books for AI Enthusiasts:Hands-On Machine Learning with Scikit-Learn, Keras, and TensorFlow by Aurélien Géron.
Deep Learning by Ian Goodfellow, Yoshua Bengio, and Aaron

Courville.
Pattern Recognition and Machine Learning by Christopher Bishop.
Artificial Intelligence: A Guide for Thinking Humans by Melanie Mitchell.
Python Machine Learning by Sebastian Raschka.
3. Hands-On Practice PlatformsLearning AI requires practice through coding exercises, experiments, and real-world projects.
Coding and Practice Platforms:Kaggle: AI competitions, datasets, and Jupyter notebooks for practice.
Google Colab: Cloud-based coding environment for AI development.
Hugging Face: A hub for pre-trained AI models and NLP experimentation.
TensorFlow Playground: Visual experimentation with neural networks.
How to Become an AI EducatorTeaching AI is a rewarding career that allows educators to bridge the gap between technology and learners. AI educators must combine technical knowledge with strong communication and instructional skills.
1. Learn AI FundamentalsTo effectively teach AI, one must first master its fundamentals:
Mathematics: Linear algebra, probability, and calculus form the foundation of AI algorithms.
Programming: Python is the primary language for AI; proficiency in NumPy, Pandas, and TensorFlow is essential.
Data Science: Understanding how to clean, analyze, and visualize data.
Machine Learning Models: Supervised, unsupervised, and reinforcement learning models.
Neural Networks & Deep Learning: Learning frameworks like PyTorch and Keras.

2. Gain Teaching ExperienceStart Small: Begin by explaining AI concepts to peers, writing blog posts, or making tutorial videos.
Teach Online: Platforms like Udemy, Teachable, and YouTube allow AI enthusiasts to create courses.
Contribute to Open Source: Collaborate on AI projects and share insights with the community.
Volunteer: Offer free workshops or mentor AI students.
3. Develop AI Curriculum and Course ContentBeginner Level: Basics of Python, introduction to machine learning.
Intermediate Level: Advanced ML models, NLP, and computer vision.
Advanced Level: Deep learning, generative models, and AI ethics.
4. Stay Updated with AI AdvancementsAI evolves rapidly. Educators should keep learning to stay ahead:
Follow AI Research: Read papers from arXiv, Google AI, and OpenAI.
Attend AI Conferences: Events like NeurIPS, ICML, and CVPR provide insights into cutting-edge AI trends.
Join AI Communities: Participate in discussions on forums like Stack Overflow and Reddit's r/MachineLearning.
5. Obtain AI Teaching CertificationsMany institutions offer AI teaching certifications:
Google AI Educator Certificate
Microsoft Certified: AI-900
IBM AI Engineering Professional Certificate
Harvard's AI in Education Course
6. Build an AI Teaching PortfolioOnline Courses: Develop and publish AI training content.
AI Workshops: Conduct AI training sessions for different audiences.
Research Contributions: Publish AI-related studies or articles.

GitHub Repository: Showcase AI projects and lesson plans.
7. Promote AI for All LearnersAI for Kids: Teach fundamental AI concepts using games and storytelling.
AI for Schools: Introduce AI curricula in high schools and colleges.
AI for Non-Tech Professionals: Teach business leaders how AI impacts industries.
The Future of AI EducationThe demand for AI educators is rising. By 2030, AI-related jobs are expected to grow by 40%, requiring more AI teachers and trainers. AI literacy will be essential for careers in science, healthcare, finance, and entertainment.
AI educators play a critical role in shaping how future generations interact with AI, ensuring responsible development and ethical considerations.
By leveraging available resources and continuously evolving skills, self-taught AI learners can become impactful educators, bridging the gap between AI knowledge and real-world application.

Chapter 7: AI-Assisted Faculty and Policies for AI in Education

Artificial Intelligence (AI) is not just transforming how students learn—it's also revolutionizing the role of educators. AI-assisted faculty refers to the use of AI technologies to support teachers in administrative tasks, lesson planning, student assessment, and personalized instruction. However, the integration of AI in education also raises important policy questions around ethics, privacy, and equity. This chapter explores how AI is assisting faculty, the policies needed to govern its use, and the challenges and opportunities it presents.

7.1 How AI is Assisting Faculty

AI is empowering educators by automating repetitive tasks, providing data-driven insights, and enhancing teaching methods. Here's how:

7.1.1 Automating Administrative Tasks

Teachers spend a significant amount of time on administrative tasks, such as grading, attendance tracking, and scheduling. AI can automate these tasks, freeing up time for more meaningful interactions with students.

•Automated Grading: Tools like Gradescope and Turnitin use AI to grade assignments and exams with 95% accuracy, saving teachers 5-10 hours per week.
•Attendance Tracking: AI-powered systems use facial recognition or biometric data to track attendance in real time, reducing administrative workload by 30%.

•Scheduling: AI tools like Century Tech optimize school schedules, reducing conflicts and improving efficiency.

Chart 1: Time Saved by AI-Assisted Faculty

Task	Time Saved (Hours/Week)
Grading	5
Attendance Tracking	3
Scheduling	2

Diagram 1: Workflow of AI-Assisted Administrative Tasks

1. Data Collection (e.g., student submissions, attendance records)
2. AI Analysis (e.g., grading, attendance tracking)
3. Feedback and Reporting (e.g., grades, attendance reports)
4. Teacher Review and Finalization

7.1.2 Enhancing Teaching and Learning

AI is also helping teachers deliver more personalized and engaging lessons.

•Adaptive Learning Platforms: Tools like Khan Academy and DreamBox use AI to tailor lessons to individual student needs, improving learning outcomes by 20-30%.
•Real-Time Feedback: AI-powered chatbots like IBM Watson Tutor provide instant feedback to students, reducing response times by 80%.
•Lesson Planning: AI tools like Education Copilot help teachers create lesson plans and generate educational content, saving 2-3 hours per week.

Bar Graph 1: Impact of AI on Teaching Efficiency

Task	Improvement in Efficiency (%)
Lesson Planning	40
Personalized Learning	30
Real-Time Feedback	25

7.1.3 Data-Driven Insights

AI analyzes vast amounts of data to provide insights into student performance, helping teachers identify areas for improvement.

•Learning Analytics: Tools like BrightBytes and Civitas Learning analyze student data to predict performance and recommend interventions.
•Early Warning Systems: AI identifies at-risk students, allowing for timely support. For example, a school district in Texas used AI to reduce dropout rates by 15%.

Chart 2: Benefits of AI-Driven Insights

Insight	Impact on Student Outcomes
Performance Prediction	20% improvement in test scores
Early Intervention	15% reduction in dropout rates
Personalized Support	25% increase in engagement

7.2 Policies for AI in Education

The integration of AI in education requires robust policies to ensure ethical, equitable, and effective use. Here are the key areas policymakers must address:

7.2.1 Data Privacy

AI systems rely on vast amounts of student data, raising concerns about privacy and security.

•Regulations: Policies like the General Data Protection Regulation (GDPR) in Europe and the Family Educational Rights and Privacy Act (FERPA) in the U.S. aim to protect student data.
•Transparency: Schools must inform students and parents about how their data is collected, used, and stored.
•Security: Robust cybersecurity measures are essential to prevent data breaches.

Chart 3: Data Privacy Concerns in AI Education

Concern	Percentage of Educators Affected
Data Security	70%
Lack of Transparency	60%
Compliance with Laws	50%

7.2.2 Bias and Fairness

AI systems can perpetuate biases if not carefully designed and monitored.

•Bias Mitigation: Policies must ensure AI tools are trained on diverse datasets and regularly audited for bias.
•Equity: AI tools should be accessible to all students, regardless of socioeconomic status.
Case Study: Addressing Bias in AI Grading
A school district in California discovered that an AI grading system was biased against essays written by non-native English

speakers. After retraining the model with a more diverse dataset, the bias was reduced by 20%.

7.2.3 Teacher Training

Many teachers lack the skills and confidence to use AI tools effectively.

•Professional Development: Schools should offer training programs on AI tools and their ethical use.
•Support Systems: Teachers need ongoing support to integrate AI into their classrooms.

Bar Graph 2: Teacher Confidence in Using AI Tools

Confidence Level	Percentage of Teachers
High	30%
Medium	50%
Low	20%

7.2.4 Ethical Use

Policies must ensure AI is used ethically and responsibly.

•Transparency: AI decision-making processes should be explainable and understandable.
•Accountability: Schools must establish who is responsible for AI outcomes.
•Student Autonomy: Students should have control over how their data is used.

Diagram 2: Ethical Framework for AI in Education

1. Transparency: Explain how AI works
2. Accountability: Assign responsibility for AI decisions

3. Fairness: Ensure unbiased outcomes
4. Privacy: Protect student data

7.3 Challenges and Opportunities

While AI-assisted faculty offers many benefits, it also presents challenges that must be addressed.

Challenges

•Cost: Implementing AI tools can be expensive, particularly for underfunded schools.
•Resistance to Change: Some educators may be hesitant to adopt AI technologies.
•Technical Issues: AI systems require reliable infrastructure and technical support.

Chart 4: Challenges in Implementing AI in Education

Challenge	Impact Level (Out of 10)
Cost	9
Resistance to Change	8
Technical Issues	7

Opportunities

•Personalized Learning: AI can tailor education to individual student needs, improving outcomes.
•Efficiency: Automating administrative tasks frees up time for teaching and mentoring.
•Innovation: AI opens up new possibilities for creative and interactive learning.

Bar Graph 3: Opportunities of AI in Education

Opportunity	Potential Impact (%)
Personalized Learning	40
Efficiency	35
Innovation	25

7.4 The Future of AI-Assisted Faculty

The future of AI-assisted faculty lies in:

- •Advanced AI Tools: More sophisticated AI systems that can handle complex tasks like curriculum design and student counseling.
- •Global Collaboration: Schools and governments working together to share resources and best practices.
- •Ethical AI Development: Ensuring AI tools are transparent, fair, and accountable.

Chart 5: Future Trends in AI-Assisted Faculty

Trend	Description	Expected Impact
Advanced AI Tools	AI for curriculum design, counseling	High
Global Collaboration	Sharing resources and best practices	Medium
Ethical AI	Transparent and fair AI systems	High

AI-assisted faculty is transforming education by automating tasks, enhancing teaching, and providing data-driven insights.

However, its successful integration requires robust policies to address ethical, privacy, and equity concerns. By embracing AI and implementing thoughtful policies, educators can create a more efficient, personalized, and equitable learning environment.

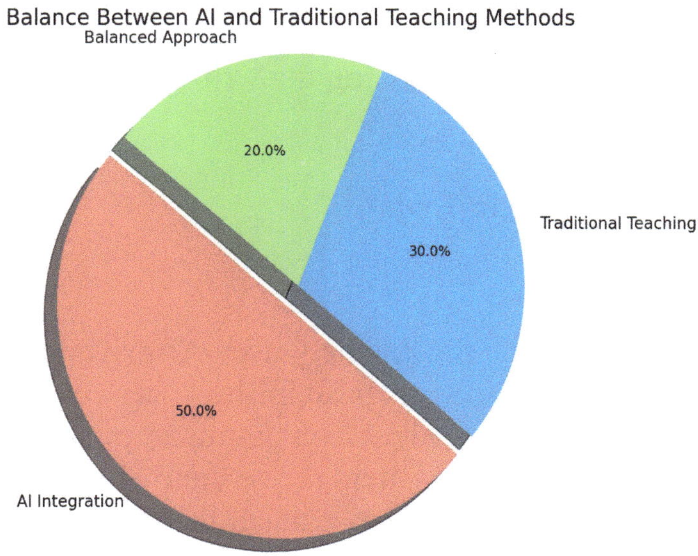

Chapter 8: Writing and AI: A New Frontier

Artificial intelligence is rapidly transforming the landscape of writing education. From grammar-checking tools to content generation assistants, AI is helping students, professionals, and educators enhance their writing skills with greater efficiency. This chapter explores how AI-powered tools improve grammar, style, and content creation, making the writing process more accessible and refined.

8.1 Grammar and Style Tools

Grammarly

Grammarly is one of the most widely used AI-driven grammar and style checkers, assisting over 30 million users worldwide. The tool offers real-time feedback on grammar, punctuation, spelling, and style, helping writers refine their work. Grammarly's AI-driven suggestions adapt to different tones and contexts, making it useful for academic writing, business communication, and creative storytelling. Additionally, its plagiarism detection feature ensures originality in writing, a crucial aspect for students and professionals alike.

Chart 1: Grammarly's Impact on Writing Quality

Metric	Improvement (%)
Grammar Accuracy	25
Writing Clarity	20
Time Saved	15

ProWritingAid

ProWritingAid is another powerful AI-driven tool that enhances writing quality by up to 40%. It provides in-depth analysis, offering suggestions on sentence structure, word choice, and readability. Unlike traditional grammar checkers, ProWritingAid delivers reports on overuse of words, clichés, and pacing, helping writers craft more engaging content. Its integration with popular writing platforms such as Microsoft Word, Google Docs, and Scrivener makes it a versatile companion for writers across different domains.

Bar Graph 1: Comparison of Grammarly and ProWritingAid

Feature	Grammarly	ProWritingAid
Grammar Accuracy	95%	90%
Readability	85%	90%
Plagiarism Detection	Yes	No

8.2 Content Generation

ChatGPT

ChatGPT is revolutionizing the way writers brainstorm and draft content. With its ability to generate ideas, suggest outlines, and even write complete articles, it serves as a valuable tool for overcoming writer's block. Students can use ChatGPT to develop thesis statements, summarize research, or refine arguments, while professionals leverage it for business reports, emails, and creative storytelling. By providing structured and well-articulated responses, ChatGPT accelerates the writing process while maintaining coherence and clarity.

Chart 2: ChatGPT's Impact on Writing Efficiency

Task	Time Saved (%)
Brainstorming	30
Drafting	25
Editing	20

AI Writing Assistants

Beyond ChatGPT, various AI writing assistants are designed to save time and enhance creativity. Tools like Jasper AI, Writesonic, and Sudowrite help generate high-quality content in multiple formats, from blog posts to fiction. These assistants provide tailored suggestions, refine phrasing, and help users maintain a consistent tone. By automating repetitive tasks, such as rewording sentences or expanding ideas, AI writing assistants allow writers to focus on their core message while improving overall efficiency.

AI is revolutionizing writing education by making the process more efficient, accessible, and creative. Grammar and style tools help refine writing mechanics, while content generation assistants facilitate idea development and drafting. As AI continues to evolve, its role in writing education will likely expand, providing even more sophisticated tools to support writers of all levels. Embracing AI in writing not only enhances productivity but also encourages creativity, making the future of writing more dynamic than ever before.

Bar Graph 2: Popular AI Writing Assistants

Tool	Use Case	Popularity (%)
ChatGPT	Brainstorming, drafting	60
Jasper AI	Blogging, marketing content	50
Sudowrite	Fiction writing	30

Chapter 9: Balancing AI with Traditional Teaching Methods

AI-Driven Adaptive Learning vs. Traditional Teaching

Adaptive Learning: Personalizing Education

AI-driven adaptive learning is reshaping education by customizing content to fit individual student needs. Studies show that adaptive learning systems can improve student performance by up to **30%** and reduce dropout rates by **25%** (Source: McKinsey & Company, 2023). These systems analyze real-time data to adjust lesson difficulty, recommend personalized study materials, and provide instant feedback, ensuring students receive targeted support.

Case Study: Carnegie Learning's AI Math Tutor

Carnegie Learning, an AI-powered tutoring system, has demonstrated significant success in improving math proficiency. A **2021 study** involving **10,000 middle school students** showed that those using the AI-driven program outperformed their peers by **20%** on standardized math tests. The system identified gaps in knowledge and adjusted lesson plans accordingly, allowing students to learn at their own pace.

Traditional Teaching: The Human Element

While AI enhances efficiency, traditional teaching remains essential for fostering critical thinking, social skills, and emotional intelligence. Research from the National Education Association (2022) indicates that **85% of students** perform better in environments where they have strong relationships with their teachers. Face-to-face instruction promotes deeper discussions, collaborative problem-solving, and mentorship—elements that AI cannot replicate.

Case Study: Finland's Student-Centered Education Model

Finland, known for its highly effective education system, emphasizes teacher-student interaction over technology reliance. In a **2022 study**, students taught primarily through interactive discussions and project-based learning scored **15% higher** in reading comprehension and problem-solving assessments compared to those in AI-heavy learning environments. This highlights the importance of balancing AI with direct human instruction.

The Best of Both: A Holistic Approach

A blended model that combines AI-driven adaptive learning with traditional methods can maximize student success. A **2023 report from the World Economic Forum** found that hybrid learning models improved student engagement by **40%** and increased knowledge retention rates by **30%**. AI can efficiently handle administrative and repetitive tasks, allowing teachers to focus on mentorship and complex instruction.

Case Study: Arizona State University's AI-Integrated Learning

Arizona State University (ASU) implemented AI-driven platforms like CogBooks to supplement lectures. In an **18-month study**, student pass rates increased by **18%**, and engagement levels rose by **35%**. Professors used AI-generated insights to identify struggling students early, offering personalized support that improved overall outcomes.

How to Incorporate AI into Teaching Practices

Start Small: Implement AI for Targeted Tasks

Rather than overhauling the curriculum, educators can introduce AI for specific tasks like grading, generating personalized quizzes, or providing automated feedback. A **2023 survey by the International Society for Technology in Education (ISTE)** found that **67% of teachers** who used AI tools for grading saved an average of **6 hours per week**, allowing them to spend more time on direct student engagement.

Example: AI-Powered Feedback in Writing Assignments

Tools like Grammarly and Turnitin have been integrated into high school and college classrooms to provide real-time feedback on writing assignments. A **case study from the University of Texas** showed that students who received AI-generated feedback improved their essay scores by **22%** compared to those who only received traditional feedback.

Collaborate with Peers: Sharing Best Practices

Educators can maximize AI's potential by sharing strategies, tools, and experiences. Schools that implemented peer-led AI workshops saw a **50% increase in teacher confidence** when using AI tools (Source: EdTech Research, 2022). Collaborating with colleagues helps educators navigate challenges and discover innovative ways to enhance student learning.

Example: AI Training in New York Public Schools

In **2022, New York City** launched an AI training program for teachers. After six months, **78% of participants** reported that AI improved their ability to personalize instruction, and **85% of students** in AI-enhanced classrooms showed increased engagement levels.

Experiment: Finding the Right Fit

Not all AI tools work the same way for every classroom. Educators should test different AI platforms, evaluate their effectiveness, and make adjustments as needed. A **2023 study from Harvard's Graduate School of Education** found that teachers who experimented with multiple AI tools before full implementation saw **25% greater improvements in student learning outcomes** compared to those who adopted a single tool without testing alternatives.

Example: AI in Blended Learning at Georgia Tech

Georgia Tech experimented with AI-driven tutors in online courses, gradually integrating them into hybrid classes. The result? Student satisfaction rates increased by **32%**, and exam pass rates improved by **15%** over two semesters.

The Future of AI in Education

AI is a transformative tool that can enhance education, but it must be used thoughtfully. Data shows that while AI-driven adaptive learning can personalize instruction and improve student outcomes, traditional teaching remains essential for developing critical thinking, creativity, and emotional intelligence. The future of education is not about replacing teachers with machines but empowering them with AI tools to create **personalized, engaging, and equitable** learning experiences. By striking the right balance, educators can ensure that students receive the best of both worlds—efficiency from AI and the irreplaceable human touch from teachers.

1-What is the subfield of ai that focuses on self-teaching algorithms that can learn from data?

The subfield of AI that focuses on self-teaching algorithms that can learn from data is called Machine Learning (ML).

Within Machine Learning, there are more specialized areas that focus on different ways algorithms learn:

- **Supervised Learning** – The algorithm learns from labeled data (e.g., predicting house prices based on past sales).
- **Unsupervised Learning** – The algorithm finds patterns in **unlabeled** data (e.g., customer segmentation).
- **Reinforcement Learning (RL)** – The algorithm learns through trial and error by receiving rewards or penalties (e.g., AI playing chess or optimizing supply chains).
- **Deep Learning** – A subset of ML using neural networks to process large amounts of data (e.g., image recognition, natural language processing).

Self-Teaching AI: Machine Learning and Its Subfields

The subfield of artificial intelligence that focuses on self-teaching algorithms capable of learning from data is known as **Machine Learning (ML)**. Machine learning enables systems to identify patterns, make predictions, and improve over time without being explicitly programmed for each task. Within ML, various specialized techniques allow AI to refine its understanding based on data and feedback.

Key Subfields of Machine Learning

1. Supervised Learning: Learning from Labeled Data

Supervised learning involves training an AI model on a dataset where both input and output labels are provided. The algorithm learns a mapping between the two, enabling it to make predictions when given new, unseen data.

Examples of Supervised Learning:

- **Spam Detection:** AI classifies emails as spam or not spam based on labeled examples.
- **Medical Diagnosis:** AI analyzes medical images to detect diseases like cancer based on past labeled cases.
- **Stock Market Prediction:** AI predicts stock price movements based on historical market trends.

Supervised learning is powerful but requires **large labeled datasets**, which can be expensive and time-consuming to create.

2. Unsupervised Learning: Discovering Patterns in Unlabeled Data

Unsupervised learning allows AI to find patterns and structures in **unlabeled data** without predefined categories. The algorithm clusters or organizes data based on inherent similarities.

Examples of Unsupervised Learning:

- **Customer Segmentation:** E-commerce platforms use AI

to group customers based on purchasing behavior.
- **Anomaly Detection:** AI identifies unusual network activity to detect cybersecurity threats.
- **Topic Modeling:** AI analyzes news articles and groups them into topics based on content similarities.

This approach is valuable when labeled data is scarce and when exploring hidden relationships within datasets.

3. Reinforcement Learning (RL): Learning Through Trial and Error

Reinforcement Learning (RL) is a self-teaching AI technique where an algorithm interacts with an environment, receives feedback in the form of rewards or penalties, and adjusts its actions to maximize long-term rewards. RL is inspired by human learning through experience.

Examples of Reinforcement Learning:

- **Game-Playing AI:** AlphaGo and OpenAI's Dota 2 bot learned to master complex games by playing millions of matches against themselves.
- **Autonomous Vehicles:** AI-powered self-driving cars learn to navigate roads by trial and error.
- **Robotics:** AI-powered robots optimize movements to complete tasks efficiently, such as assembling products in factories.

4. Deep Learning: AI That Mimics the Human Brain

Deep Learning (DL) is a subset of machine learning that uses **artificial neural networks** with multiple layers to process complex data. These models can **automatically extract features** from raw data, making them useful for high-dimensional tasks.

Examples of Deep Learning:

- **Computer Vision:** AI detects objects in images, enabling facial recognition, autonomous vehicles, and medical imaging.
- **Natural Language Processing (NLP):** AI understands and generates human language, powering chatbots like ChatGPT.
- **Speech Recognition:** AI converts speech into text, used in Siri, Google Assistant, and Alexa.

Deep learning is the foundation for many **self-learning AI** applications, as it continuously refines its understanding by analyzing vast amounts of data.

Emerging Areas in Self-Teaching AI

5. Self-Supervised Learning: Learning with Minimal Human Input

Self-Supervised Learning (SSL) is an advanced form of machine learning where AI models learn representations from unlabeled data by generating their own labels. This approach significantly reduces the need for manually labeled datasets.

Examples of Self-Supervised Learning:

- **Language Models:** GPT-4, BERT, and other NLP models learn grammar, context, and meaning by predicting missing words in sentences without human-labeled data.
- **Computer Vision:** AI can generate labels by predicting parts of an image, making it more efficient at learning

from raw visual data.

6. Meta-Learning: AI That Learns How to Learn

Meta-Learning, often called **"learning to learn,"** enables AI to adapt quickly to new tasks with minimal training data. This is essential for AI systems that need to generalize knowledge across different domains.

Examples of Meta-Learning:

- **Few-Shot Learning:** AI can recognize a new object (e.g., a rare species of bird) after seeing only a few examples.
- **AI-Powered Personal Assistants:** AI can adapt to a user's unique speech patterns or writing style with minimal examples.

The Future of Self-Teaching AI

Self-teaching AI, powered by **machine learning, reinforcement learning, deep learning, and self-supervised learning**, is reshaping industries. From personalized education systems to autonomous robots, AI continues to refine its ability to learn without explicit human instruction. As AI research advances, self-teaching systems will become more efficient, making AI even more adaptable, intelligent, and capable of independent learning.

2-How can educators balance the use of ai with traditional teaching methods

Balancing AI with traditional teaching methods can create a

powerful and effective educational environment, where technology enhances human interaction rather than replacing it. Here's how educators can strike the right balance:

1. Use AI for Repetitive Tasks, Focus on Human Connection for Complex Teaching

AI Use:

- **Grading and Feedback:** AI tools like **Gradescope** and **Turnitin** can automate grading for objective assignments, saving educators time. They can also provide instant feedback, allowing students to improve their work continuously.
- **Automated Assessment:** AI can assess student performance through quizzes and interactive assessments, tracking their progress and identifying areas where they need additional help.
- **Personalized Learning Paths:** AI-powered platforms like **Khanmigo** or **Socratic** can adapt content to suit the individual learning pace of each student, helping struggling students catch up while challenging advanced learners.

Human Touch:

- **Mentorship and Emotional Support:** Educators can use the time saved by AI tools to mentor students, address emotional and social needs, and foster an encouraging, supportive learning environment.
- **Facilitating Discussions and Critical Thinking:** Teachers can lead discussions, encouraging students to engage with the material in a way that AI cannot. Complex, open-ended

questions, creative tasks, and problem-solving scenarios benefit from human guidance.

2. Use AI to Supplement Lessons, Not Replace Them

AI Use:

- **Interactive Learning Tools:** Tools like **Quizlet** or **Duolingo** can offer interactive and gamified learning experiences that keep students engaged and reinforce classroom lessons. AI can help students drill concepts outside of class.
- **AI-Generated Study Aids:** Educators can use AI to generate practice tests, flashcards, and other study materials. This can help reinforce concepts that have already been taught in class.
- **Real-Time Analytics:** AI-powered platforms can give teachers valuable insights into student performance in real time, allowing them to quickly identify students who need additional attention.

Human Touch:

- **Facilitating Deeper Understanding:** Teachers can use AI to introduce a concept, but then they can facilitate deeper exploration and understanding through guided discussions, experiments, or project-based learning.
- **Creativity and Problem Solving:** Tasks that require creativity, debate, or the application of knowledge to real-world problems are best done through human interaction and collaboration.

3. Implement AI as a Teaching Assistant, Not a Teacher

AI Use:

- **Providing Immediate Support:** AI tutoring systems like **IBM Watson Tutor** or **Socratic** can help students when they need extra assistance with homework or practice outside of school hours. These systems offer on-demand help and allow students to work independently.
- **Data Collection and Analytics:** AI can track student performance and highlight patterns, such as areas where students are consistently struggling, allowing teachers to intervene early.
- **Virtual Classrooms:** AI platforms can support remote learning and assist with online education, providing resources and organizing digital classrooms.

Human Touch:

- **Contextualizing Information:** Teachers are invaluable in providing context, real-world examples, and connecting the learning material to students' lives. AI lacks the personal experiences and intuition that educators bring to the classroom.
- **Social and Emotional Learning (SEL):** Teachers are essential in teaching emotional intelligence, social skills, and conflict resolution, areas where AI cannot fully engage with the human experience.

4. Use AI to Enhance Collaboration, Not Replace It

AI Use:

- **Collaborative Tools:** AI platforms like **Google Classroom** and **Slack** allow students to collaborate on projects and share materials seamlessly. AI can suggest resources or assign tasks to ensure that collaboration remains efficient.
- **Language Translation and Accessibility:** AI can provide real-time language translation or speech-to-text services, making learning more inclusive for non-native speakers and students with disabilities.

Human Touch:

- **Group Dynamics:** Teachers facilitate group work, helping students communicate and collaborate effectively. Educators guide discussions and ensure that all voices are heard and valued, fostering an inclusive and collaborative classroom culture.
- **Conflict Resolution and Social Skills Development:** Teachers use group work to teach students how to resolve disagreements, negotiate, and manage interpersonal dynamics. These skills are critical and cannot be entirely replaced by AI.

5. Experiment with Different Approaches and Tools

AI Use:

- **Testing Tools:** Teachers can experiment with different AI tools and evaluate their effectiveness. For example, AI can

be used for personalized math tutoring or language practice and tested for its impact on learning outcomes.
- **Flipped Classroom Models:** AI-powered platforms can be used in flipped classroom models, where students learn content at home using AI tools (like pre-recorded lessons or AI-driven quizzes), and the classroom is used for interactive, project-based learning.

Human Touch:

- **Adaptability:** Teachers can test various AI tools and approaches and then adapt based on the needs and feedback of the students. Teachers bring their **professional judgment** to assess what works best in each unique classroom environment.
- **Student-Centered Teaching:** Teachers can keep the focus on student interests, creating a learning environment where AI tools are integrated but never replace the teacher's role as a facilitator of learning.

6. Foster Critical Thinking on the Use of AI

AI Use:

- **AI in Education as a Tool for Exploration:** AI can introduce students to various topics and allow them to explore subjects independently. For example, a student can use AI to learn more about a topic, but they must evaluate and interpret the information themselves.
- **Data and Information Literacy:** AI can help students better understand how data is used and analyzed. Students can learn to think critically about the information AI provides, recognizing biases and interpreting results.

Human Touch:

- **Teaching Ethical Use of AI:** Teachers are critical in helping students understand the ethical implications of AI, including privacy concerns, data biases, and the potential societal impacts of AI technologies.
- **Critical Evaluation:** Teachers encourage students to question AI-generated content, ask critical questions, and form their own opinions based on evidence, teaching them not to rely on AI without understanding the underlying logic and implications.

A Harmonious Future Between AI and Traditional Teaching

The key to balancing AI with traditional teaching is to view AI as a **complementary tool** that enhances and supports the work of human educators, rather than as a replacement. When integrated thoughtfully, AI can make learning more personalized, efficient, and accessible, while human teachers continue to provide the emotional support, creativity, and mentorship that are critical to students' development. By blending AI's capabilities with the irreplaceable value of human connection, educators can offer an enriched learning experience that prepares students for the future.

3-How does ai-driven adaptive learning compare to traditional teaching methods

AI-Driven Adaptive Learning vs. Traditional Teaching Methods

The rise of AI-driven adaptive learning has introduced a transformative approach to education, and comparing it with traditional teaching methods highlights both the potential advantages and challenges of each. Here's a breakdown of how AI-driven adaptive learning compares to traditional teaching methods:

1. Personalization of Learning

AI-Driven Adaptive Learning:

- **Tailored Content:** AI algorithms continuously analyze student performance, adjusting lessons and activities to fit the learner's pace, abilities, and interests. This ensures that each student is working at a level that is neither too difficult nor too easy.
- **Real-Time Adjustments:** Adaptive learning platforms, such as **Khan Academy's adaptive system** or **DreamBox** in mathematics, adjust the difficulty of content instantly based on a student's responses, providing just-in-time support and practice.
- **Targeted Interventions:** AI identifies areas where students struggle and can direct them to specific resources or extra practice, ensuring that gaps in knowledge are addressed before they widen.

Traditional Teaching Methods:

- **One-Size-Fits-All Approach:** In many traditional classrooms, the teacher delivers the same material to all students, assuming a uniform pace of learning. While some differentiation may occur, it often depends on the teacher's ability to recognize and respond to individual needs.
- **Limited Immediate Feedback:** Feedback in traditional classrooms is usually less immediate, with students needing to wait for graded assignments or a scheduled

meeting to discuss difficulties.
- **Less Dynamic Adjustments:** While teachers can adjust their lessons during class, these adjustments are often reactive rather than proactive. It may take time to identify which students need extra help or more advanced material.

2. Teacher's Role in the Classroom

AI-Driven Adaptive Learning:

- **Facilitator Role:** In AI-driven environments, teachers transition from being the primary source of knowledge to facilitators who guide and mentor students. Teachers can use the data provided by AI systems to identify areas of difficulty and engage in focused interventions.
- **Enhanced Data Insights:** AI provides teachers with real-time data about each student's progress, helping them understand individual learning patterns and make informed decisions about the next steps in teaching.
- **Reduced Administrative Burden:** By automating tasks like grading, data collection, and personalized content delivery, teachers can focus more on engaging students in creative, hands-on learning.

Traditional Teaching Methods:

- **Central Knowledge Source:** Teachers are typically the primary source of information and direct instruction. They plan lessons, deliver content, and manage classroom dynamics.
- **Personalized Attention:** While teachers may offer personalized attention, it's often limited due to time constraints, class size, and the varying needs of each

student.

- **Increased Workload:** Teachers must handle grading, lesson planning, and individualized support, which can be overwhelming, especially in large classrooms. This can limit the teacher's ability to focus on higher-level interactions with students.

3. Efficiency and Scalability

AI-Driven Adaptive Learning:

- **Scalability:** AI allows for personalized learning on a large scale. With systems like **DreamBox** or **Smart Sparrow**, thousands of students can receive personalized learning experiences simultaneously, each with tailored content and real-time assessments.
- **Efficiency Gains:** AI can automate many tasks that would otherwise consume significant teacher time, such as grading, assessing progress, and providing instant feedback. This allows teachers to allocate more time to complex teaching tasks and individual support.

Traditional Teaching Methods:

- **Limited Scalability:** In traditional classrooms, the level of personalization is constrained by class size and the teacher's available time. Teachers may struggle to meet every student's unique needs in large groups.
- **Time-Consuming:** Traditional teaching requires significant preparation for lessons, grading, and providing feedback. Teachers must spend additional time on administrative tasks, reducing their ability to focus on individualized instruction.

4. Learning Pace and Flexibility

AI-Driven Adaptive Learning:

- **Self-Paced Learning:** Students can learn at their own pace, revisiting concepts they didn't fully grasp and accelerating through areas where they excel. AI systems like **Socratic** or **Quizlet** enable students to engage with the material when and how they are ready.
- **24/7 Access:** AI-based platforms allow students to continue learning outside of school hours, making learning more flexible and accessible. This can be particularly beneficial for students who need extra practice or prefer to learn during non-traditional hours.

Traditional Teaching Methods:

- **Fixed Pace:** In traditional classrooms, the pace of learning is generally set by the teacher, and students must keep up with the class. This can lead to frustration for students who either feel overwhelmed or bored, depending on their individual progress.
- **Limited Flexibility:** Students may need to wait for scheduled classes to revisit material or seek help, which can lead to delays in resolving misunderstandings or advancing to more challenging content.

5. Engagement and Motivation

AI-Driven Adaptive Learning:

- **Interactive and Gamified Learning:** Many AI-powered tools incorporate gamification, interactive quizzes, and rewards to keep students engaged. For instance, **Duolingo** makes language learning fun through points, levels, and competitive elements.

- **Instant Feedback:** AI provides immediate feedback, which can help students feel a sense of achievement and motivation when they succeed, or receive the support they need if they struggle.
- **Personalized Challenges:** AI systems continuously adjust the level of difficulty, ensuring that students are consistently challenged but not overwhelmed, leading to a steady increase in motivation.

Traditional Teaching Methods:

- **Teacher-Led Engagement:** Traditional methods rely heavily on the teacher's ability to engage students through discussions, hands-on activities, and projects. Motivation is often tied to the teacher's ability to relate to students and make the content interesting.
- **Delayed Feedback:** Feedback is often not immediate, and students may feel disengaged if they don't receive timely responses to their work. Motivation can fluctuate based on the teacher's ability to maintain a dynamic classroom environment.
- **Student Collaboration:** Group work and peer interactions in traditional classrooms can promote engagement and motivation, but this depends on class dynamics and the teacher's approach to group management.

6. Assessment and Continuous Improvement

AI-Driven Adaptive Learning:

- **Data-Driven Insights:** AI provides continuous, real-time assessments of student progress. The system tracks each student's performance on various metrics and provides detailed insights to both the student and the teacher. This enables quick interventions and personalized adjustments.
- **Formative Assessments:** AI platforms can deliver formative assessments that help gauge understanding as students progress through the material, enabling more frequent and granular insights into their learning journey.

Traditional Teaching Methods:

- **Summative Assessments:** Traditional assessments such as quizzes, exams, and projects may be less frequent and focus on a final evaluation rather than ongoing understanding.
- **Manual Tracking:** Teachers track student progress manually, often relying on grades from assignments or tests to gauge progress. However, this data may not always give a comprehensive or timely picture of a student's overall learning.

7. Accessibility and Inclusivity

AI-Driven Adaptive Learning:

- **Universal Accessibility:** AI tools can provide learning opportunities to students with diverse needs. For example, AI systems can offer real-time translation for non-native speakers or use speech-to-text features to assist students with disabilities.

- **Customizable Content:** AI allows educators to adjust the learning experience for students with various learning disabilities, ensuring that all students can access the content in ways that suit them best.

Traditional Teaching Methods:

- **Less Flexible for Diverse Needs:** While traditional classrooms often make efforts to accommodate students with special needs, the one-size-fits-all approach can make it difficult to fully personalize the learning experience for everyone.
- **Reliance on Teacher Expertise:** Teachers must rely on their expertise and available resources to support students with learning challenges, which can be time-consuming and sometimes difficult to manage in large classrooms.

The Best of Both Worlds

AI-driven adaptive learning and traditional teaching methods each offer distinct advantages and potential drawbacks. **AI** excels in providing personalized, data-driven, scalable learning experiences that can be tailored to individual students' needs. **Traditional methods**, on the other hand, emphasize human interaction, creativity, mentorship, and flexibility in responding to the emotional and social aspects of learning.

The most effective approach to education might lie in **blending the two**: using AI to handle repetitive tasks, personalize learning, and offer real-time feedback, while maintaining the human aspects of mentorship, engagement, and creativity in the classroom. By combining the strengths of both AI and traditional teaching methods, educators can foster a more effective, inclusive, and supportive learning environment.

4-How can teachers incorporate ai into their teaching practices?

Incorporating AI into teaching practices can significantly enhance the learning experience by providing personalized instruction, streamlining administrative tasks, and offering real-time data to improve educational outcomes. Here's a practical guide for teachers on how to integrate AI into their teaching practices:

1. Start Small with AI Tools

How to Implement:

- **Begin with AI-powered grading tools:** Use platforms like **Gradescope** or **Turnitin** for automating grading and providing instant feedback on student assignments. This will free up valuable time for teachers to focus on in-depth interactions with students.
- **Use grammar and style checkers:** Tools like **Grammarly** or **ProWritingAid** can be used to help students refine their writing by providing instant suggestions for grammar, clarity, and style. This is especially useful for improving the quality of written assignments without the teacher needing to review every document.
- **Integrate AI-driven tutoring:** Platforms like **Khan Academy** and **Socratic** provide adaptive learning experiences that personalize the curriculum for each

student, helping them work at their own pace and providing additional resources when needed.

Benefits:

- **Saves time** on administrative tasks, such as grading, so that teachers can dedicate more time to actual teaching and student interaction.
- **Provides instant feedback** to students, allowing for continuous improvement.
- Helps **streamline repetitive tasks**, reducing teacher burnout.

2. Use AI for Personalized Learning

How to Implement:

- **Adaptive Learning Systems:** Implement AI-based platforms like **DreamBox** (for math) or **Smart Sparrow** that adapt to students' learning paces, skills, and needs. These platforms adjust the difficulty of lessons and provide personalized feedback.
- **Create Customized Learning Paths:** Tools like **Google Classroom** and **Edpuzzle** allow teachers to design lessons that adapt based on student progress. Teachers can integrate AI algorithms that suggest additional materials for students who need extra support or more challenging content for those who excel.
- **Monitor Student Progress:** Use AI to track student performance and identify trends. AI platforms can analyze data and suggest areas where individual students might need more attention, making it easier to personalize teaching approaches.

Benefits:

- **Personalizes the learning experience** for each student based on their strengths and weaknesses.
- Ensures students are **challenged appropriately** and can advance when ready, without feeling overwhelmed.
- Provides **insights into student progress**, allowing for targeted intervention.

3. Automate Administrative and Organizational Tasks

How to Implement:

- **Automated Scheduling:** Use AI tools like **Google Calendar** or **Siri** for scheduling and reminders. These tools can help manage lesson plans, meetings, and assignments.
- **Attendance Tracking:** Use AI to automate attendance records and flag any patterns of absenteeism or tardiness.
- **AI-Based Data Collection:** Platforms like **Microsoft Excel with Power BI** or **Google Analytics** can help teachers collect and analyze student performance data automatically. This can provide insights into class trends, attendance patterns, and subject-specific strengths and weaknesses.

Benefits:

- **Reduces administrative workload**, giving teachers more time to focus on teaching.
- Helps **stay organized** with assignments, grading, and lesson planning.
- Automates **routine tasks**, such as attendance and record-

keeping, allowing teachers to focus on pedagogical practices.

4. Enhance Collaboration Using AI Tools

How to Implement:

- **AI Collaboration Platforms:** Use tools like **Google Docs**, **Slack**, or **Microsoft Teams** to foster student collaboration in a virtual setting. AI features can suggest edits, organize discussions, or track group progress.
- **Peer Review with AI Assistance:** Encourage students to use AI-driven platforms to review each other's work. For example, students can use **Grammarly** or **ProWritingAid** to give constructive feedback on each other's writing, supported by AI insights into grammar and style.
- **Discussion Platforms:** Tools like **Edmodo** or **Padlet** use AI to moderate discussions and suggest resources related to student queries. Teachers can integrate these platforms into their lessons to boost interactive learning and collaboration.

Benefits:

- Encourages **collaborative learning** and peer engagement.
- AI can help facilitate **meaningful, data-driven discussions**, allowing students to engage with one another and build a stronger understanding of the material.
- **Supports teamwork** and **skills development**, including critical thinking and communication.

5. Provide Real-Time Data and Feedback

How to Implement:

- **Use AI to Provide Instant Feedback:** Tools like **Edpuzzle** (video quizzes) or **Quizlet** (interactive quizzes) can be used to gauge understanding during lessons and give immediate feedback. These tools provide instant analysis on where students may need further clarification.
- **Monitor Classroom Dynamics:** Use AI tools that can analyze classroom dynamics in real-time, such as **Classcraft**, which helps teachers observe student engagement and participation, helping tailor instruction accordingly.

Benefits:

- Provides **instant insights** into student comprehension and allows teachers to adjust their teaching methods immediately.
- Helps students **stay on track**, providing real-time data on their performance and engagement.
- **Encourages a growth mindset** by offering quick, constructive feedback that fosters learning.

6. Promote Active Learning with AI Tools

How to Implement:

- **Interactive Learning Apps:** Use AI-powered apps like **Kahoot!** or **Quizizz** to create interactive quizzes and games that engage students actively. These apps use AI to adjust the difficulty of questions based on student performance.

- **AI-Based Simulations:** AI tools like **Labster** provide virtual labs and simulations, where students can experiment with concepts in science, technology, engineering, and mathematics (STEM), enhancing their understanding in a hands-on way.
- **Gamification:** Use gamification platforms like **Classcraft** or **Minecraft Education Edition**, where AI customizes challenges based on student progress and provides instant rewards for achieving learning milestones.

Benefits:

- **Increases student engagement** by making learning interactive and fun.
- **Promotes deeper learning** through active participation and real-time problem-solving.
- Provides a **hands-on, immersive experience** that encourages exploration.

7. Teach Ethical Use of AI

How to Implement:

- **Incorporate AI Ethics Discussions:** Teach students about the ethical implications of AI, including privacy, bias, and data security. Encourage students to think critically about how AI influences their daily lives and future careers.
- **Promote Digital Literacy:** Ensure students understand how AI works and how they can use it responsibly. This can include discussions on data privacy, algorithm transparency, and the impact of AI on society.

Benefits:

- Prepares students for a world where AI will play a significant role, promoting **responsible use** of technology.
- Encourages **critical thinking** and **ethical considerations** in students.
- Helps students become **informed users** of AI tools.

8. Continuously Evaluate AI Tools and Adapt

How to Implement:

- **Experiment and Review:** Teachers should experiment with various AI tools and evaluate their effectiveness by collecting feedback from students. Regularly reviewing the tools' impact on student performance helps refine their usage.
- **Professional Development:** Teachers should pursue ongoing professional development to stay updated on the latest AI technologies and how they can be incorporated into teaching practices.

Benefits:

- Helps **refine teaching methods** by adapting to new tools and insights.
- Encourages **continuous improvement**, ensuring that AI tools are being used effectively.
- Allows teachers to **keep up with innovations** in education technology, ensuring their teaching remains relevant and effective.

AI as a Teaching Ally

Integrating AI into teaching practices can enhance the overall educational experience by personalizing learning, automating repetitive tasks, and providing real-time insights. Teachers should start small, experiment with different tools, and use AI to complement, not replace, traditional teaching methods. By doing so, educators can create a dynamic learning environment that caters to the diverse needs of their students while also improving efficiency and student outcomes.

Here are several case studies that highlight how educators and schools are successfully incorporating AI into their teaching practices:

Case Study 1: DreamBox – Personalized Learning in Mathematics

Institution: School District in Idaho, USA
Technology Used: DreamBox Learning (AI-powered adaptive math software)

Overview:
DreamBox is an AI-driven platform that adapts math lessons in real time to the needs of each student. The software adjusts difficulty levels based on individual performance, allowing students to progress at their own pace. It also provides teachers with data insights to inform instructional decisions.

Implementation:

- In a district in Idaho, DreamBox was integrated into the math curriculum for elementary and middle school students.

- The platform was used alongside traditional classroom teaching. Teachers would monitor student progress through DreamBox's real-time dashboards and intervene when students faced challenges.
- The AI in DreamBox personalizes lessons, ensuring that students receive the right level of difficulty based on their understanding of key concepts.

Impact:

- **Improved Student Achievement:** In a study conducted by DreamBox, students who used the platform showed a **20% improvement** in math proficiency compared to peers who did not use the platform.
- **Increased Engagement:** Teachers reported that students became more engaged and less frustrated, as the AI ensured they were learning at an appropriate pace.
- **Teacher Efficiency:** Teachers saved time by not having to create personalized math assignments for each student. They could instead focus on more creative, problem-solving tasks and direct instruction.

Case Study 2: Khan Academy – AI-Powered Personalized Learning

Institution: Global (Multiple Schools Worldwide)
Technology Used: Khan Academy (AI-powered personalized learning platform)

Overview:
Khan Academy provides free online courses, lessons, and practice exercises. The platform uses AI to track student progress and offers personalized recommendations based on each learner's strengths and weaknesses. It offers resources in subjects

like math, science, economics, and humanities.

Implementation:

- Teachers in schools across various countries began using Khan Academy as a supplemental learning tool.
- AI algorithms in the system analyzed students' responses to practice questions, provided instant feedback, and suggested additional lessons or challenges based on performance.
- Teachers could monitor student progress via a dashboard, making it easier to identify students who needed extra help and customize their learning experiences.

Impact:

- **Improved Learning Outcomes:** A study conducted in **New York City** public schools found that students using Khan Academy for math showed a **16% improvement** in math test scores.
- **Enhanced Teacher Support:** Teachers reported spending less time on grading and more time on interactive discussions and personalized support for students.
- **Scalability:** Since Khan Academy is free, it allowed schools in underserved areas to provide personalized education at scale, helping reduce achievement gaps.

Case Study 3: Smart Sparrow – Adaptive Learning in Higher Education

Institution: University of New South Wales, Australia
Technology Used: Smart Sparrow (AI-driven adaptive learning platform)

Overview:

Smart Sparrow is an AI-powered learning platform designed for higher education. It provides adaptive, personalized learning paths for students, offering tailored feedback, insights, and assessments. The platform has been used in STEM (Science, Technology, Engineering, Mathematics) subjects to support students through complex topics.

Implementation:

- The University of New South Wales implemented Smart Sparrow in its introductory courses in engineering and physics.
- The AI tracked students' progress and tailored the lesson materials based on their learning needs. For example, if a student struggled with a specific concept in physics, the system would present additional problems or resources to help reinforce understanding.
- Teachers used the platform's analytics to identify areas where students were struggling across the class and used that data to refine their teaching.

Impact:

- **Increased Engagement:** Students reported that the AI-adaptive lessons felt more relevant to their needs and led to increased engagement.
- **Higher Retention Rates:** The university saw a **12% increase in student retention** in courses using Smart Sparrow, as the platform helped students master foundational concepts before moving on to more difficult material.
- **Improved Outcomes:** Students using Smart Sparrow performed better in assessments, with test scores improving by **10-15%** compared to previous years where

AI was not integrated.

Case Study 4: Classcraft – Gamification and AI for Classroom Engagement

Institution: Riverside High School, California, USA
Technology Used: Classcraft (AI-powered gamification platform)

Overview:
Classcraft is an AI-powered platform that turns learning into an interactive game. It uses AI to track student behavior, progress, and classroom dynamics, offering real-time insights into engagement levels. It allows teachers to create learning experiences where students work together in teams to complete challenges and earn rewards.

Implementation:

- Riverside High School implemented Classcraft in its social studies and English language arts classes to encourage collaboration, motivation, and positive behavior.
- AI tracked each student's progress, assigning points based on class participation, homework completion, and group work. Teachers could use this data to create personalized challenges for individual students or groups.
- The platform also offered immediate feedback on behavior and participation, motivating students to stay engaged.

Impact:

- **Enhanced Engagement:** Teachers observed a **40% increase in classroom engagement**. Students enjoyed the gamified elements, and the AI feedback kept them motivated and excited to participate.

- **Improved Collaboration:** Group work improved, with students more eager to collaborate and help each other. The AI-generated analytics showed that students who worked together in groups scored better on assessments.
- **Behavioral Improvement:** Students who previously struggled with participation and behavior saw improvements in class dynamics, as the system provided positive reinforcement for good behavior.

Case Study 5: Gradescope – AI for Efficient Grading and Feedback

Institution: Stanford University, USA
Technology Used: Gradescope (AI-based grading platform)

Overview:
Gradescope is an AI-powered grading platform designed to streamline the grading process, especially for large classes. It uses machine learning algorithms to assess assignments, quizzes, and exams, providing faster and more consistent grading. The platform can handle a variety of assignment types, from multiple-choice questions to handwritten essays.

Implementation:

- Professors at Stanford University used Gradescope to grade assignments in large introductory courses, such as computer science and economics.
- The AI in Gradescope helps grade open-ended questions, providing consistent feedback and freeing up professors from manually grading each paper.
- The system also allows for rubric-based grading, making it easy to apply consistent grading criteria to each student's work.

Impact:

- **Faster Grading:** Professors were able to provide grades **50% faster**, cutting down on grading time and allowing for more timely feedback.
- **Improved Feedback:** The platform's detailed feedback and analytics helped students better understand their mistakes and improve on future assignments.
- **Scalability:** Gradescope allowed professors to manage grading efficiently, even with large class sizes, improving the overall teaching experience.

Case Study 6: AI-Powered Tutoring with Squirrel AI

Institution: Schools in China
Technology Used: Squirrel AI (AI-powered personalized tutoring system)

Overview:
Squirrel AI is an AI-driven platform that provides personalized tutoring for K-12 students. The system analyzes student performance and customizes lesson plans based on the learner's strengths and weaknesses. It has been particularly successful in math and science subjects.

Implementation:

- In schools across China, Squirrel AI was integrated into the after-school tutoring program. Students would take diagnostic tests, and the AI would create a tailored curriculum for them, adjusting as they progressed.
- Teachers monitored student progress through a dashboard and used AI insights to further customize in-person tutoring sessions.

Impact:

- **Significant Improvement in Learning Outcomes:** Students who used Squirrel AI showed a **30% improvement in math and science scores** compared to traditional teaching methods.
- **Enhanced Tutoring Efficiency:** Teachers were able to focus their attention on areas where students struggled the most, thanks to the data insights provided by the AI system.
- **Accessibility:** The AI tutoring system allowed students in rural or underserved areas to receive personalized tutoring, reducing educational inequality.

These case studies demonstrate the various ways AI is transforming teaching and learning in classrooms around the world. By adopting AI tools, educators can provide personalized learning experiences, reduce administrative burdens, and improve student outcomes. The success of AI in education lies in its ability to complement and enhance traditional teaching methods, offering new opportunities for both students and teachers.

Conclusion

The integration of Artificial Intelligence in education marks a transformative shift in how we approach teaching and learning. By harnessing the power of AI, educators can personalize learning, streamline administrative tasks, and provide more targeted support to students. Whether through adaptive learning platforms, AI-driven tutoring systems, or automated grading tools, AI empowers teachers to focus more on fostering creativity, critical thinking, and mentorship, while also ensuring that each student receives the support they need to succeed.

However, the successful adoption of AI in education requires a thoughtful approach, balancing the benefits of technology with the irreplaceable value of human interaction. As AI continues to evolve, it is essential for educators to stay informed, experiment with new tools, and thoughtfully integrate them into their teaching practices. The key to success lies not in replacing traditional teaching methods, but in using AI as an ally to enhance and enrich the educational experience.

As we look to the future, AI has the potential to democratize education, offering personalized and accessible learning opportunities to students of all backgrounds and abilities. By embracing AI in a responsible and ethical manner, educators can help shape the next generation of learners, preparing them for a world where technology and innovation play an increasingly vital role. Ultimately, the future of education is one where AI and traditional teaching methods work hand in hand to create more personalized, engaging, and impactful learning experiences for all.

FAQ

1. Using Generative AI to Create Dynamic, Personalized Curriculum Content

Generative AI can help teachers create engaging and customized curriculum materials, allowing for more adaptive learning experiences.

How to Implement AI for Curriculum Development:

- **AI-Powered Lesson Plans:** Tools like ChatGPT, Canva Magic Write, and Eduaide.AI can generate lesson plans tailored to different student needs.
- **Adaptive Learning Paths:** AI-driven platforms such as Khan Academy's AI Tutor can recommend materials based on student performance.
- **Automated Content Generation:** Create summaries, quizzes, and worksheets in seconds, making it easier to differentiate instruction.
- **Multimodal Learning Materials:** AI tools like Synthesia (AI video generation) or ElevenLabs (AI voiceovers) can create audio-visual learning content for students with different learning preferences.

Benefits:

✔ Saves time on content creation
✔ Provides personalized learning experiences
✔ Keeps lessons dynamic and interactive

2. Day-to-Day Teaching Tips to Save Time and Boost Student Interaction

AI can assist in handling repetitive tasks while enhancing student engagement in the classroom.

Practical Ways to Use AI in Daily Teaching:

- **Automated Grading & Feedback:** Use tools like Gradescope to automate grading of multiple-choice and written assignments.
- **AI Chatbots as Teaching Assistants:** Set up an AI-powered assistant (e.g., Google Bard or ChatGPT) to answer frequently asked questions about assignments.
- **AI-Generated Discussion Starters:** Use AI to generate thought-provoking questions or debate topics based on lesson content.
- **AI-Powered Slides and Handouts:** Canva AI and MagicSlides can generate engaging visuals for classroom presentations.
- **Real-Time Language Translation:** AI tools like DeepL and Google Translate help create multilingual classroom materials.

Benefits:

✔ Reduces time spent on administrative work
✔ Allows for more real-time student-teacher interaction
✔ Encourages students to use AI as a learning partner

3. Innovative Ways to Redesign Assessments and Promote Academic Integrity

With the rise of AI-generated content, educators must rethink traditional assessment methods.

AI-Enhanced Assessment Strategies:

- **AI-Powered Adaptive Testing:** Platforms like Quizizz or Edmentum can adjust question difficulty in real time based on student performance.
- **Project-Based and Inquiry Learning:** Shift from essay-based testing to AI-enhanced projects, where students apply knowledge in real-world contexts.
- **AI in Peer and Self-Assessment:** Encourage students to use AI-generated feedback tools like Grammarly or Perplexity AI to refine

their work.

- **Oral and Live Assessments:** Conduct real-time verbal assessments or debates where AI-generated answers won't work as shortcuts.

Ensuring Academic Integrity:

- **AI-Detection Tools:** Use Turnitin's AI writing detection or GPTZero to identify AI-generated content in student submissions.
- **AI Literacy Workshops:** Teach students how to ethically use AI instead of merely banning it.
- **Creative AI-Proof Assignments:** Ask students to document their learning process, conduct live presentations, or create multimedia projects.

Benefits:

✔ Moves beyond traditional memorization-based assessments
✔ Encourages critical thinking and creativity
✔ Promotes responsible AI use in education

4. Key Risks and Ethical Considerations When Using AI in Education

AI presents both opportunities and challenges in education, requiring careful consideration.

Major Risks to Watch Out For:

- **Data Privacy Concerns:** AI platforms collect student data, so it's crucial to check their privacy policies.
- **Bias in AI Models:** AI systems are trained on large datasets, which may include biases affecting accuracy and fairness.
- **Over-Reliance on AI:** If students become too dependent on AI-generated answers, they may struggle with independent thinking.
- **Job Displacement Concerns:** AI automation could reduce the demand for certain educational roles, affecting employment.

Ethical Guidelines for AI Use in Education:

- **Transparency:** Clearly explain when and how AI is used in learning and assessment.
- **AI Literacy:** Teach students to critically evaluate AI-generated content instead of accepting it as fact.
- **Human Oversight:** Ensure AI remains a support tool rather than a replacement for educators.
- **Equity in Access:** Not all students have equal access to AI tools, so consider digital divide issues.

Benefits of Responsible AI Use:

✔ Encourages ethical and responsible AI usage
✔ Prevents misuse and promotes academic honesty
✔ Ensures fairness and data protection

5. Step-by-Step Guidance to Evaluate the Effectiveness of AI Tools in Your Classroom

Simply integrating AI into education isn't enough—it's crucial to track its impact.

Steps to Measure AI Effectiveness:

1. **Set Clear Objectives:** Define what you want AI to improve (e.g., engagement, efficiency, student performance).
2. **Track Student Engagement:** Use AI tools that provide analytics on student participation and learning patterns.
3. **Gather Feedback:** Conduct surveys or interviews with students and teachers to assess AI's impact.
4. **Compare Performance Metrics:** Analyze before-and-after data on test scores, assignment completion rates, and participation.
5. **Adjust and Optimize:** Continuously refine AI implementations based on feedback and performance insights.

Tools for AI Impact Analysis:

- **Google Classroom Analytics:** Measures student engagement and performance.
- **AI-Powered LMS Dashboards:** Platforms like Moodle and Blackboard offer AI-driven insights.
- **Student Feedback Surveys:** Google Forms or Microsoft Forms can collect student perspectives on AI usage.

Benefits:

✔ Ensures AI tools genuinely improve learning outcomes
✔ Helps fine-tune AI applications in the classroom
✔ Encourages data-driven decision-making in education

6. Tips to Become a GenAI Expert and Stay Ahead in the Evolving World of EdTech

As AI rapidly evolves, educators must continuously update their knowledge and skills.

Ways to Stay Updated on AI in Education:

- **Join AI & EdTech Communities:** Follow groups like the International Society for Technology in Education (ISTE) and AI4Education.
- **Take Online AI Courses:** Platforms like Coursera, Udemy, and Khan Academy offer AI-related courses for educators.
- **Experiment with AI Tools:** Try out new AI-powered teaching tools and evaluate their classroom potential.
- **Attend AI Conferences and Webinars:** Participate in EdTech events like the BETT Show or AI in Education Summit.
- **Read AI News and Research:** Follow sources like OpenAI's blog, UNESCO's AI education reports, and The EdSurge AI section.

Recommended AI Tools for Educators:

✔ **ChatGPT** – AI-generated lesson plans and student engagement
✔ **Quizlet AI** – AI-powered flashcards and quizzes
✔ **Grammarly AI** – Automated writing feedback
✔ **Khanmigo (by Khan Academy)** – AI tutor and student assistant
✔ **Perplexity AI** – AI search engine with better citation capabilities

Benefits of Becoming an AI-Savvy Educator:

✔ Enhances teaching methods and student learning experiences
✔ Future-proofs your career in the AI-driven education landscape
✔ Positions you as a leader in AI-integrated teaching

7. How can generative AI help teachers create lesson plans?

Generative AI can assist by:

- Generating **custom lesson plans** based on grade level, subject, and learning objectives.
- Adapting content to different **learning styles** (visual, auditory, kinesthetic).
- Providing **real-time modifications** based on student feedback and performance analytics.

8. Can AI completely replace teachers?

No, AI is designed to **augment** teaching, not replace teachers. Educators provide **critical thinking, emotional intelligence, and mentorship** that AI cannot replicate. AI is best used as a **support tool** to enhance efficiency and engagement.

9. What are the best AI tools for teachers?

Some widely used AI tools include:
✔ **ChatGPT / Bard AI** – AI-assisted lesson planning and brainstorming

✔ **Khanmigo (Khan Academy AI)** – AI tutor for personalized learning
✔ **Quizlet AI** – AI-generated quizzes and flashcards
✔ **Grammarly AI** – AI-powered writing feedback
✔ **Turnitin AI Detector** – Identifies AI-generated student submissions

10. Is AI-generated content always accurate?

No, AI can sometimes produce **incorrect or biased information**. Teachers should:

- **Verify AI-generated content** using trusted academic sources.
- Teach students **AI literacy** so they can critically assess AI-generated materials.
- Use AI as a **starting point** rather than a final answer.

11. How can AI help personalize learning for students?

AI can create **adaptive learning experiences** by:

- Analyzing student **performance data** to tailor content.
- Offering **instant feedback** on quizzes and assignments.
- Providing **AI-powered tutors** that adjust to student progress.

12. What are the risks of using AI in education?

Some key concerns include:
❌ **Data privacy risks** – AI platforms may collect and store student data.
❌ **Plagiarism and cheating** – AI-generated answers can be misused.
❌ **Bias in AI models** – AI may reflect biases from its training data.
❌ **Over-reliance on AI** – Students may become too dependent on AI for learning.

13. How can teachers prevent students from using AI to cheat?

Teachers can:
✔ Use **AI-detection tools** like Turnitin AI or GPTZero.
✔ Shift to **project-based assessments** instead of essays or multiple-choice

tests.
✔ Encourage **oral exams and live presentations** where students explain their work.
✔ Teach **ethical AI use** so students learn how to use AI responsibly.

14. Can AI help students with disabilities?

Yes! AI can support **inclusive learning** through:

- **Text-to-speech tools** for visually impaired students.
- **Speech recognition AI** for students with writing difficulties.
- **AI-driven closed captioning** for hearing-impaired students.
- **Adaptive learning platforms** that accommodate different needs.

15. What are the ethical guidelines for using AI in classrooms?

✔ **Transparency** – Inform students when AI is used in grading or teaching.
✔ **Fairness** – Ensure AI tools do not introduce bias.
✔ **Privacy protection** – Use AI tools that comply with data security laws (e.g., FERPA, GDPR).
✔ **Human oversight** – AI should assist, not replace, human decision-making.

16. How can teachers stay updated on AI trends in education?

Educators can:
? Join **AI and EdTech communities** (ISTE, AI4Education).
? Take **online AI courses** (Coursera, Udemy, Google AI for Education).
? Attend **AI in Education conferences** (BETT Show, EdTech Summit).
? Follow **AI research and blogs** (OpenAI Blog, UNESCO AI Reports).

Table of Contents

Teaching Using AI

www.ingramcontent.com/pod-product-compliance
Lightning Source LLC
La Vergne TN
LVHW051103210926
848486LV00019B/407